Recipes from Differer

by Julie Garnett

Section 1: Drinks and Ice Cream Treats
Banana Lassi – India   2
Tropical Fruit Punch – Africa   4
Ginger Beer – Caribbean   6
Strawberry Milkshake – USA   8
Knickerbocker Glory — USA   10

Section 2: Sandwiches
Cheese and Tomato Sandwich – UK   12
Croque Monsieur – France   14
Peanut Butter and Jelly Sandwich – USA   16
Seafood Open Sandwich – Scandinavia   18
Tuna and Salad Pitta – Middle East   20

Section 3: Traditional Sweets and Puddings
Pancakes – UK   22
Honey Cakes, or "Katarzynki" – Poland   24
Sweets for the Piñata – Mexico   27

Glossary   32

WARNING! Always ask an adult for help when you use kitchen equipment, such as a sharp knife, a tin opener or a grater. Also ask for help when you are using a hot grill or oven and remember to wear oven gloves.

Longman

Edinburgh Gate
Harlow, Essex

Banana Lassi – India

It can get very hot in India, so people like to drink lots of cold drinks like this one called lassi. Lassis are made from fruit, water and yoghurt. In the big cities you can buy lassi from stalls in the streets. A lassi will cool you down after a hot curry.

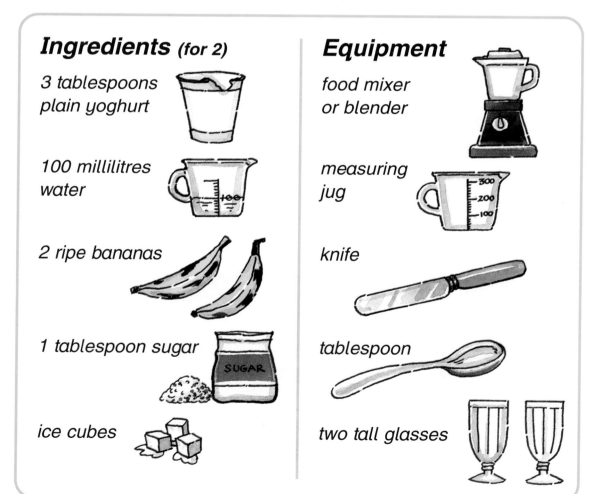

Ingredients (for 2)

3 tablespoons plain yoghurt

100 millilitres water

2 ripe bananas

1 tablespoon sugar

ice cubes

Equipment

food mixer or blender

measuring jug

knife

tablespoon

two tall glasses

What to do

1 Fill the jug with water up to the 100 millilitres mark.

2 Add four or five ice cubes and let them melt up to the 150 millilitres mark.

3 Peel and cut the bananas into slices.

4 Put the water, yoghurt, bananas and sugar into the mixer or blender. Mix until it is smooth.

5 Pour the lassi into two tall glasses and serve.

Tropical Fruit Punch – Africa

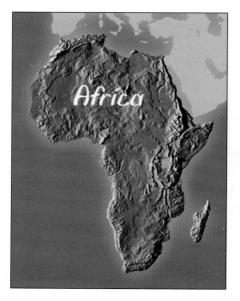

Oranges, mangoes, bananas, pineapple and kiwi are tropical fruit.

They grow all over Africa in the wild and on farms. They are used in all sorts of food and drink like fruit salad or a drink called "punch". Fruit punch is drunk at special times like at a wedding or when a baby is given its name.

Ingredients

1 banana

1 orange

1 kiwi fruit

1 apple

200 millilitres orange juice

100 millilitres pineapple juice

500 millilitres lemonade

ice cubes

Equipment

sharp knife

chopping board

large bowl

measuring jug

What to do

1 Peel the fruit and slice into rings. Put them in the bowl.

2 Measure out the fruit juices and pour them on top of the fruit.

3 Measure out the lemonade and pour it into the bowl. Stir to mix.

4 Add ice cubes to chill the punch.

Ginger Beer – Caribbean

Ginger and sugar cane are crops grown in the Caribbean where it is very hot. They are used to make a cold ginger beer drink that people like at Carnival.

Ingredients

100 grams root ginger

2 litres water

sugar to taste

Equipment

small sharp knife

grater

large glass bowl

sieve

jug

bottles

What to do

1 Peel the ginger with a sharp knife.

2 Grate it. (Mind your fingers!)

3 Put the grated ginger into the bowl and pour the water on top.

4 Leave it to stand overnight.

5 Strain the liquid through a sieve into a jug. Add sugar to taste.

Throw away the ginger bits.

6 Pour the ginger beer into bottles.

Keep in the fridge.

Strawberry Milkshake – USA

Children in the USA love ice cold milkshakes. They make them at home or they buy them in milk bars or soda shops – cafés, which sell mainly pop and milkshakes. A real milkshake should have fresh fruit and ice cream in it, like this recipe.

Ingredients

12 strawberries

250 millilitres cold milk

2 large dollops of strawberry ice cream (taken out of the freezer to soften)

Equipment

knife

large bowl

whisk

measuring jug

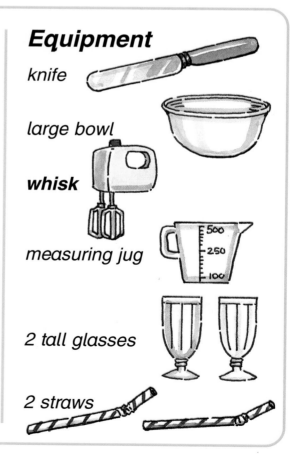

2 tall glasses

2 straws

What to do

1 Wash the strawberries and cut them in half. Put them in the bowl.

2 Measure out the milk and pour it into the bowl.

3 Add the ice cream.

4 Whisk it up until all the lumps have gone and it is nice and frothy.

5 Carefully pour the milkshake into two tall glasses. Put in straws and suck! Mmmmmmm!

Knickerbocker Glory – USA

This is another recipe from the USA with ice cream in it. Special cafés called ice cream parlours were very popular in America in the 1950s. They sold all sorts of ice creams, including this fancy one. You need a long spoon to get right down to the bottom of the glass!

What is a knickerbocker glory and how did it get its wonderful name?

It is a large and fancy ice cream sundae that is served in a tall glass shaped like this.

The glass looks a bit like the shape of baggy trousers men wore in the 19th century. They were tied below the knee. They were called "knickerbockers" after Diedrich Knickerbocker, an American.

A knickerbocker glory is made of different kinds of ice cream in layers with fruit, syrup, and a topping of nuts. This recipe uses tinned fruit. You could have peaches, raspberries or strawberries. Choose your favourite.

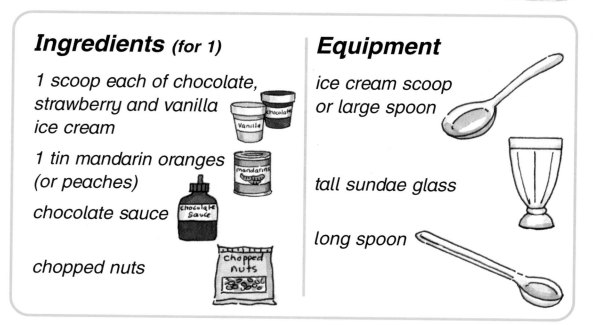

Ingredients (for 1)

1 scoop each of chocolate, strawberry and vanilla ice cream

1 tin mandarin oranges (or peaches)

chocolate sauce

chopped nuts

Equipment

ice cream scoop or large spoon

tall sundae glass

long spoon

What to do

1 Put the scoop of chocolate ice cream at the bottom of the glass.

2 Put a spoonful of mandarins or peaches on top and a **drizzle** of chocolate sauce.

3 Now add the strawberry ice cream, more fruit and more sauce.

4 Repeat with the vanilla ice cream.

5 Top with chocolate sauce and sprinkle some nuts over it.

6 Eat with the long spoon. Enjoy!

Cheese and Tomato Sandwich – UK

Sandwiches are a popular snack for lunch all around the world, but especially in England where they were invented. They can be made of white or brown bread. They can have all sorts of fillings, such as cheese, meat, salad, bananas or jam.

Sandwiches got their name because the first sandwich was made for John Montagu, the Earl of Sandwich, about 250 years ago. He asked for a snack he could eat while he was playing cards. His servant put a slice of beef between two pieces of bread so that he would not need a knife and fork.

Ingredients (for 1)

2 slices bread

butter

cheese

1 tomato

Equipment

knife

grater

plate

What to do

1 Spread the butter thinly on each slice of bread.

2 **Grate** the cheese.

3 Cover one slice of bread with the grated cheese.

4 Cut the tomato into four slices. Lay them on top of the cheese.

5 Cover the tomato with the second slice of bread. Press together firmly.

6 Cut the sandwich in half and serve on a plate.

Croque Monsieur – France

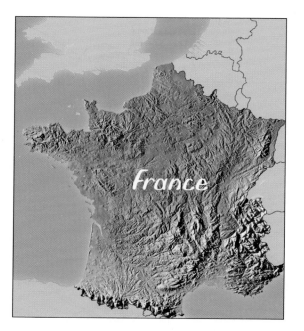

French children love toasted cheese and ham sandwiches called "Croque-monsieur". You can buy them at cafés and snack bars all over France. They make them using French cheese called "Gruyère". Our version uses English Cheddar cheese.

Ingredients (for 1)

Cheddar cheese

2 slices bread

1 slice ham

butter or margarine

Equipment

grater

knife

grill pan

oven gloves

What to do

1 First take out the grill pan and then preheat the grill.

2 **Grate** the cheese while the grill is getting hot.

3 Toast one side of both slices of bread and then spread butter or margarine thinly on the untoasted side of the bread.

4 Put the slice of ham on top of one slice of bread and cover with the other slice.

Keep the toasted sides outside.

5 Lay the cheese on top of the sandwich.

6 Put the sandwich back under the grill and cook until the cheese melts.

Peanut Butter and Jelly Sandwich – USA

This sandwich is a favourite with children in the USA. In America, jam is called "jelly". Children often take this sandwich to school for lunch.

This is how you make it.

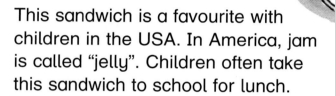

Ingredients *(for 1)*

2 slices bread

peanut butter

strawberry jam

Equipment

knife

What to do

1 Spread peanut butter on one slice of bread.

2 Spread strawberry jam on the other slice.

3 Sandwich the slices together. Press firmly.

4 Cut in half.

5 Enjoy! Yum, yum!

Seafood Open Sandwich – *Scandinavia*

In Scandinavian countries (Sweden, Denmark and Norway) sandwiches do not have a piece of bread on top of the filling like a lid, so they are called "open" sandwiches. Layers of fish, meat and salad vegetables are put on top of a slice of bread and butter. They often use rye bread, which is dark brown and tastes nutty.

Ingredients *(for 2)*

tinned prawns or shrimps

2 slices bread

butter

lettuce

mayonnaise

any from: grated carrot
            cucumber slices
            sliced avocado
            onion rings

Equipment

can opener

2 plates

knife

spoon

fork

What to do

1. Start by putting a slice of bread on each plate. Butter the bread.

2. First put a layer of lettuce leaves on top of the bread.

3. Next, dollop a spoonful of mayonnaise onto the lettuce.

4. Then pile the prawns or shrimps on top.

5. Finally, **garnish** with a topping of your choice.

Note: You will need to eat this sandwich with a knife and fork.

Tuna and Salad Pitta – Middle East

Pitta bread is the main kind of bread made in the Middle East. It is a hollow flat bread which can be opened up like a pocket. It can be filled with fish, chicken, meat and/or salad. Filled pitta halves or mini-pittas are great for school lunches or picnics.

Here is a recipe using tuna. You can leave out any of the salad ingredients you don't like.

Ingredients *(for 2)*

1 pitta

1 small tin tuna

mayonnaise or salad cream

lettuce leaves

1 tomato

slices of cucumber

Equipment

sharp knife

tin opener

small bowl

dessertspoon

What to do

1   Ask an adult to open the tin of tuna for you.
    Tip the tuna into the bowl.

2   Add a dessertspoon of mayonnaise or
    salad cream and mix it with the tuna.

3   Cut the pitta in half
    across the middle.
    Carefully split
    each half open to
    make two pockets.

4   Tear the lettuce leaves into little pieces.
    Put a few in each pocket. Add some slices
    of tomato then some cucumber.

5   Finish with the tuna mayonnaise mixture.
    Spoon in as much as you can.

Pancakes – UK

Pancake Day used to be called Shrove Tuesday. It comes just before Lent when Christians give up something they enjoy. Pancakes were made to use up the eggs and flour so that people could have a feast before they started to fast for the 40 days leading up to Easter. Some places in England have a pancake race every year. Some hold competitions for tossing pancakes.

Ingredients
(for about 6)

50 grams plain flour

pinch of salt

1 egg

150 millilitres milk

oil for frying

Utensils

sieve

large bowl

whisk or fork

measuring jug

weighing scales

small frying pan

What to do

1 First **sift** the flour and salt into the bowl.

2 Next make a dip in the middle of the flour and break the egg into it.

3 Whisk with the fork or whisk, adding the milk gradually, a little at a time.

4 When you have a smooth batter, leave it to stand for about 30 minutes.

5 Ask an adult to help you cook the pancakes as you need hot oil and a very hot pan.

Optional fillings and toppings:

- lemon juice and sugar
- jam (warmed)
- runny honey
- maple syrup and ice cream
- fruit, such as peaches, raspberries, stewed apple

Honey Cakes, or "Katarzynki" – Poland

The 6th of December is Saint Nicholas' Day in Poland. Saint Nicholas puts a present under children's pillows while they are asleep. He also leaves katarzynki at the foot of the bed. These are little honey cakes made in a special shape for Christmas.

Ingredients

200 grams honey
(about half a jar)

1 teaspoon mixed spice

100 grams dark brown sugar

1 egg

300 grams self-raising flour

2 teaspoons baking powder

Utensils

weighing scales

a large mixing bowl

fork

sieve

wooden spoon

rolling pin

round cake cutter

greased baking sheet

pastry brush

What to do

1   Turn on the oven and set it at 200°C (gas mark 6), or 180°C for a fan oven, to heat up.

2   Put the honey, spice, sugar and egg into a large bowl. Mix with a fork until smooth.

3   Using the sieve, **sift** the baking powder and flour into the bowl.

4 Mix all the ingredients until you have a firm **dough**. Use your (clean) hands at the end.

5 On a **floured board**, **roll out** the dough to a thickness of about 1 centimetre.

6 Cut out the cakes with a round cake cutter.

7 Lay the cakes on a greased baking sheet.

8 Mix some honey with warm water in a cup and brush the cakes with it.

9 Bake for 15–20 minutes on the middle shelf of the oven.

Sweets for the Piñata – Mexico

For birthdays and at Christmas, Mexican children play a game in which they take turns to be blindfolded and try to hit a papier maché container hanging from a tree. When the container breaks, all the sweets inside fall to the ground and everyone scrambles to pick up as many as they can.

How to make a piñata

Ingredients

a balloon

petroleum jelly

old newspapers

string

Equipment

coloured tissue paper

wallpaper paste

paints

mixed wrapped sweets

What to do

1 Blow up the balloon and tie it at the neck.

2 Cover the balloon with a layer of petroleum jelly, making sure you leave no gaps.

3 Tear the newspaper into little pieces, dip into the paste and cover the balloon with a single layer. (Overlap the pieces so that there are no gaps.) Leave a small hole at the neck.

4 Now repeat this with a layer of little pieces of tissue paper.

5 Continue with alternate layers of newspaper and tissue paper until there are six layers altogether.

6 Leave to dry.

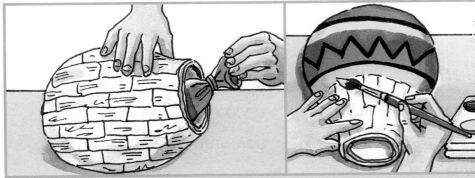

7 When the paper is completely dry, prick the balloon and take it out.

8 Paint the piñata in bright colours.

WARNING! If you prick the balloon too soon the piñata will collapse.

9 Now half-fill the piñata with sweets.

10 Make two small holes opposite each other at the top of the piñata. Thread the string through them and tie it. Ask an adult to help with this.

11 Now your piñata is ready to be hung up. Have fun!

Any kind of wrapped sweets can be used to fill the piñata.
Marzipan sweets are easy to make. Here are some ideas
to start you off.

Ingredients

1 packet of marzipan   cocoa powder

food colouring   coloured foil

box of dates

What to do

Stuffed dates

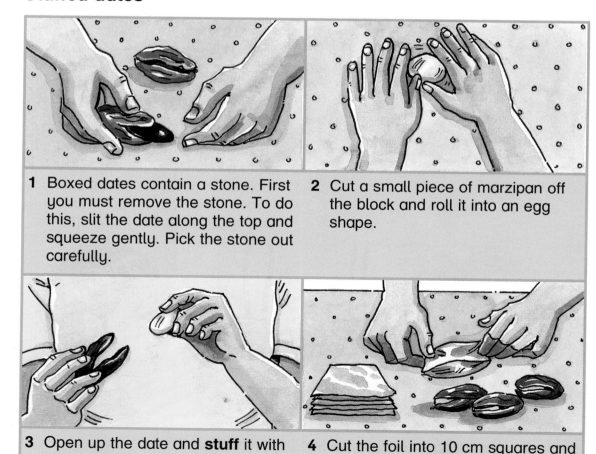

1 Boxed dates contain a stone. First you must remove the stone. To do this, slit the date along the top and squeeze gently. Pick the stone out carefully.

2 Cut a small piece of marzipan off the block and roll it into an egg shape.

3 Open up the date and **stuff** it with the marzipan.

4 Cut the foil into 10 cm squares and wrap each date in one.

Marzipan fruit

- Roll small pieces of marzipan into balls and use green food colouring for apples, red for cherries and orange for oranges. Roll in cocoa powder for potatoes.

- Other fruit shapes that are easy to make are bananas, plums or melons.

Glossary

baking sheet   a tin tray used for baking biscuits, etc.

dough   a thick mixture of flour and water or milk ready for making cakes or bread

drizzle   a thin trail of oil or sauce

floured board   a board that has had flour sprinkled over it to stop the dough from sticking

garnish   to decorate food (usually with salad or herbs)

greased   lightly covered with a thin layer of butter or margarine

grate   to rub against sharp edges to make small pieces, such as cheese or carrots

ingredients   the things that go together to make the food

pinch   the amount you can hold between your thumb and first finger, such as a pinch of salt

roll out   to use a rolling pin to roll dough or pastry out flat

sieve   a container with wire or plastic mesh at the bottom which separates lumps from powder or liquid; the lumps stay in the sieve and the liquid or powder falls through the holes

sift   to shake powder like flour through a sieve to get the lumps out

stuff   to fill completely

utensils   kitchen equipment and tools

whisk   a kitchen tool used to whip up liquid like milk or eggs until bubbly and frothy